CW01667650

Elgin

Past and Present

Compiled by
Mike Seton.
Contemporary photographs by
Gordon Brown, Alan Clarke,
Rob Donaldson-Webster and Al Moir.

SUB SPE

Moray District Council 1995

Design and layout by Graphics Section, Moray District Council.
Printed by Printing Section, Moray District Council.

New and revised edition 1995

ISBN 0 9511931 5 5

Acknowledgements

The first edition of this work appeared in 1980 at a time when, despite the developments of the late 1960s, Elgin still retained much of its traditional form. The building of the town centre relief road in 1979-81 and developments consequent upon it have brought significant changes to the appearance of the town centre. Now that, with the pedestrianisation of the central portion of the High Street, these developments are concluded it seemed an appropriate time to produce a new and revised edition.

As previously the author has drawn heavily on the staff and resources of the District Council's local studies collections in Grant Lodge for both the historic photographs and the research material. The splendid contemporary photographs were all taken by four members of the Moray Camera Club, Gordon Brown, Alan Clarke, Rob Donaldson-Webster and Al Moir.

The publication of this work was only made possible through the support of Moray District Council with funding from the Elgin Common Good Fund.

Elgin Cathedral from North College Street

The Cathedral of Moray was consecrated on this site in 1224, after having previously been at Birnie and Spynie. It had an eventful life. In 1270 it was seriously damaged by fire after which the choir was doubled in length with aisles added on each side and a Chapter House built opening off the north aisle. In 1390 it was sacked by the Wolf of Badenoch in revenge for his excommunication by the Bishop. Scarcely had it recovered from this it was attacked again, in 1402, by Alexander Macdonald of the Isles. In 1506 part of the great central tower collapsed. Over the years following the Reformation the building was at worst vandalised, at best neglected. The lead from the roof was removed in 1567 and the painted rood screen destroyed in 1640. The collapse of the mid tower in 1711 took with it the nave and the choir. It was not until 1807 that the process of decay was arrested when an enclosure wall was built. In recent years a great deal of repair and restoration work has been carried out.

Pansport and The Elgin Brewery

The Panns Port is all that remains of the defensive wall, some twelve feet high and over half a mile long which surrounded the grounds of the Cathedral, making the Chanonry, as it was called, the Bishop's own city, quite separate from neighbouring Elgin. One of the four gateways in this wall, it was more commonly known in early days as the 'Water Yet', deriving its name from the meadow land lying immediately to the east known as 'le Pannis'. The entrance was defended by both a portcullis and a pair of massive wooden doors. It was restored in 1857.

Through the archway can be seen the buildings of the Elgin Brewery. This was established in 1784 by a consortium of local businessmen who bought a piece of ground immediately to the east of the Cathedral for sixty pounds. Throughout the 19th century the brewery acquired a wide reputation for the quality of its ale, beer and porter. Although rebuilt following a fire in 1898, the business had passed its heyday and in 1912 the whole complex was bought for the town for £700 and the buildings demolished to reveal the fine view of the Cathedral we have today.

Andersons Institution

Anderson's Institution was founded through the generosity of a local boy made good. Andrew Anderson was born in extremely humble circumstances. He joined the East India Company, rising to the rankof General, making a fortune and bequeathing much of it to found the Insitution which bears his name..It was built in 1831 to a design by Archibald Simpson, the architect of St Giles Church, and provided a home for the destitute, young and old, in three distinct sections: a hospital for those over the age of 55, a School of Industry and Anderson's Free School. At its opening in 1833 it accommodated 22 boys and 18 girls between the ages of 6 and 10 and ten old people, five men and five women. The males wore suits of light grey cloth and bonnets and the females brown russet dresses. In 1891 the School of Industry was abolished. The Free School, later to become the East End School, was established 'for the education of male and female children whose parents, though in humble circumstances, are able to maintain and clothe them.' Children still boarded at Anderson's until after the Second World War, but since the last pupil left it has provided for old people only. The bequest in 1991 of a local baker, William Morrice, enabled the creation of family units on a modernised ground floor.

South College Street

The main entrance to the town from Aberdeen and the east is along South College Street. The limits of mediaeval Elgin were quite well-defined with a wall of sorts and four gateways, or ports. Hereabouts was the East Port marking the eastern boundary of the town. It was removed in 1792 along with the South Port and the Cross. This gateway possibly dated from the early fifteenth century when there was a general rebuilding following the destructive raid of the Wolf of Badenoch in 1390. In 1935 the properties on the south side of the street were demolished and this part of the town was altered still further with the construction of the town centre relief road in 1981 and the subsequent building of a superstore, opened in 1991.

WAY
COFFEE
MEALS

Museum and Little Cross

In 1402 Alexander McDonald of the Isles 'spulzied' (despoiled) the Cathedral, for which as a penance he erected a cross on this site at the west entrance in the Cathedral precinct wall.. The Little Cross consists of a fifteen feet high column on a base of four steps in the shape of a pyramid and capped by a sundial dated 1733. The sundial and the top of the column were replaced in facsimile in 1941. In the sixteenth century this was a place of punishment with stocks and a pair of jougs. Behind the Cross can be seen the buildings of the Elgin Museum. Erected in 1842 for the Elgin and Morayshire Literary and Scientific Association, the building was considerably extended in 1896 by the addition of two new halls, separated by a thin brick wall which could be removed to make one large hall if required. The award-winning museum is presently run by the Moray Society who have done much to improve the display of the exhibits in recent years. Nearby was the site of one of the town's three public wells, covered during road resurfacing as recently as 1956.

THE LEGEND

High Street - East end

The building with the tower set back from the rest is St. Giles. It occupies the site of two former houses, Old Lodge built in 1800, and the much older town house of the Cummings of Lochtervandich. All that survives from this house is a stone panel built into the wall of St. Giles bearing the arms of the Cumming and Chalmers families and the initials I.C. and I.C. and the date 1576. On the right is the well-known Braco's Banking House, built in 1694 with arched windows, which were later remodelled as plain rectangles and were only restored to their original shape in 1901.

COLLEGE·STREET
HIGH STREET

Sheriff Court

Elgin's judicial facilities were given a massive uprating in the middle of the last century. In the foreground is the Sheriff Court house designed by local architects A & W Reid and completed in 1866 shortly before Glover Street was formed immediately to the east. Adjoining the Sheriff Court are the Burgh Court buildings opened a few years earlier in 1839 on the site of the town house of the Andersons of Linkwood. Work started on a new block of council offices to replace this building in 1937, but the intervention of war and subsequent financial restrictions postponed completion until 1952.

Red Lion Close

Red Lion Close is typical of the closes in this part of town. It was fronted by the old Red Lion Inn, where, in 1773, Samuel Johnson and James Boswell dined in the course of their celebrated Tour through Scotland to the Hebrides. It was, unfortunately, the only place in the entire country where Dr Johnson 'found reason to complain of a Scottish table', not surprising if the local tradition is true that the pudding served to him had been boiled in a man's bonnet. The building fronting the Close is a fine example of the arcaded buildings for which Elgin is noted. It is inscribed with the date 1688.

59 -71 High Street

When the middle block came up for sale in 1900 it comprised two shops with houses over with houses and garden ground, i.e. a close, behind stretching back to Harveystank Road. This traditional pattern was still to be found throughout most of the town centre until the late 1960s, when the shopping development shown here was built. Its demise was finally sealed by the construction of the town centre relief road in 1981. In the 1930s one enterprising businessman had a factory behind these buildings where he produced 'Nerfl' (abbreviated from 'Never fail'), a domestic cleaner and polisher.

A.T MAYS
AMAYSING!
LATE DEALS
E351 NSE
9341 MAN

Lossie Wynd

Before the opening of North Street about 1821, Lossie Wynd was the principal entrance to the town from the north. Even then, despite being so narrow that two carts could not pass, it remained "the most crowded thoroughfare in Elgin." In early times the North Port stood about halfway up this street until its removal in July 1787. In 1916 the residents petitioned the Town Council to change its name to Union Street, 'wynd' being considered 'vulgar' by some. Only four years later, in a fit of nostalgia, the Council reverted to Lossie Wynd despite a petition from the residents not to change it back.

The floods of 1915, shown here, were the worst in the area since 1829, the whole area from Blackfriars Haugh to Newmill being one vast expanse of water with all communications between Elgin and Bishopmill being cut off.

100 HG

St. Giles from the east

The centre of Elgin is dominated by St. Giles Church. There has been a church on this site since the 12th century. In 1679 part of the roof collapsed destroying the nave. In the rebuilding that followed it seems to have been restored to its original form of a Greek cross with nave and transepts. The transepts were removed about 1740 and the chancel or 'Little Kirk' in 1800. The nave or 'Muckle Kirk' remained until 1826. In that year it was demolished to make way for the present St. Giles, designed by Archibald Simpson, the architect of Anderson's Institution. Built in the style of a Greek temple the tower, a copy of the Choragic Monument of Lysicrates in Athens, rises to some 112 feet.

NEXT
NEXT
PEDESTRIAN
ZONE
SALE

The Muckle Cross

The Muckle Cross stands a few yards to the east of St. Giles Church. There has been a market cross here since as early as 1365, although the present one is a replica of that erected in the reign of Charles I and demolished about 1792 as it had become ruinous.. The only part to survive this demolition was the Lion Rampant, which stood for many years on the walls of South College. It was returned in 1888 when a replica of the Cross was erected, the gift of one William Macandrew, a member of an old Elgin family. The interior of the upper part of the seventeenth century cross was often used by the boys of the town to hold the materials collected for a bonfire on the King's birthday. In the days before radio and television it was from the Muckle Cross that announcements of national and local importance were made.

Holiday Shop
Holiday
Holiday

The 'Tower'

There is a tradition that the building on the right, known as the 'Tower' originally belonged to the Knights of St. John. It is unlikely that the Templars ever held property in Elgin, although the Tower may have belonged at one time to Arbroath Abbey. The tower itself is the only remaining portion of the house built in 1634 by Andrew Leslie and Jean Bonyman. The building adjoining the tower was demolished in 1876. It bore the inscription 'A.L. 1629 J.B.'

The building which replaced it had its entrance through the tower which had its harling removed to restore it to its original appearance. At the same time the mouldings round the doors and windows and the coats of arms on the tower had their "modern coatings of paint" removed. The property on the left was replaced by the present building, designed by R.B. Pratt, in 1905.

DE SHOES
SALE SALE
SALE SALE

Plough Hotel / Palace Buildings

The Palace Buildings in the centre of the modern photograph were erected towards the end of the last century to house the Palace Hotel. It replaced the Plough Hotel. In 1902 when it was put up for sale the property comprised a shop fronting the High Street, the entrance to the hotel and a bar. The principal public rooms of the Hotel were on the first floor with bedrooms and servants' accommodation above. The hotel's stables extended back to South Street where, in 1855, there was said to be "sufficient room for erecting additional houses." In 1888 the licensee was charged with selling two pints of whisky to an hostler on a Sunday. Each pint cost 1s 6d. In 1970 during work on the construction of a new supermarket next door cracks appeared in the building. At that time it was used for a mixture of shops, offices and flats.

Currys
CRAWFORD'S
RESTAURANT
FREE

War Memorial / Gordon Arms

About 5,000 people were present on December 4, 1921 when Colonel Johnston of Lesmurdie unveiled Elgin's memorial to the 461 men of the town and parish who fell in the First World War. The memorial was designed by Percy Portsmouth of Edinburgh. The bronze figure holds a sword in the right hand signifying Victory and a torch in the left typifying Peace. The twelve foot high pedestal is of local Greenbrae stone and bears the names of the dead on bronze panels on three sides.

The Gordon Arms was a hostelry of considerable importance in the days before the motor-car. It operated an extensive posting business hiring horses, traps and drivers to visitors collected from the railway stations by its own horse-drawn omnibus. In these days it was the largest hotel in the town and was especially busy on market days and 'Feein' Fridays' when farmers and farm workers from miles around gathered on the Plainstones opposite. It closed down in 1980.

MACKAYS
SALE
H169 XSE

Arnotts

When A.L. Ramsay opened his new department store in 1904 on the site occupied by many of these buildings it marked a revolution in shopping in Elgin. A.L. Ramsay had started business in 1845, later being joined by his son William. William, a fine example of the Victorian work ethic, became a partner in 1869 and from that date "did not miss a day at the counters for seven years". In 1991 another shopping revolution came to Elgin with the opening f the St. Giles Centre shopping mall behind what had been Ramsay's frontage. The cast-iron drinking fountain just visible on the left was erected in 1860 from funds raised by local tradesmen. The fountain was cast by George Smith in Glasgow. It had four openings each with a ladle. Surplus water fell into troughs beneath, where horses could be watered and under these and level with the street were trays for dogs to drink from. The fountain was topped by a street light. There was said to be none other like it in Scotland.

1876
SONYA
LITTER

The Assembly Rooms

The building with the blinds and the Venetian window was built by the Trinity Lodge of Freemasons in 1821 as their Assembly Rooms. It occupied the site of Calder House, occupied in its latter days by the eccentric Dr Alexander Dougal and reputedly haunted. The Assembly Rooms was a popular social venue for many years and boasted a dance-floor said to be one of the finest in the north.. It was demolished, amid some controversy, in 1969, to make way for the present building. The contrasting views at the time were that either "the new building will improve the corner" or that it diminished the character of the town. Next to the Assembly rooms are the premises of the North of Scotland Bank erected in 1857 on the site of Drummuir House, one-time site of Elgin's Theatre Royal and replaced by the present branch of the Clydesdale Bank in 1969. The building on the right, occupied by Batchen the shoemaker, may have dated from as early as 1619 and was demolished about 1880.

OLIVERS
GRANADA
BRADFORD
&BINGLEY

The Tollbooth

The fountain was constructed in 1846 on the site of the recently demolished Tolbooth, This building which housed the court-room, council offices and town gaol, was the place where the last public execution in Moray took place when William Noble was hanged for murder on 31 May 1834 before a crowd of 500 drawn from many miles around and who behaved in a "most quiet and becoming manner". The Tolbooth had been built in 1605 using stone from the wall surrounding the kirkyard some of which had come from the fabric of the church itself when undergoing repair in the 15th century. When the Tolbooth was taken down in 1843 some of the stone was used in the construction of the Free Presbyterian Church. The old tolbooth does not seem to have been a place of great security. In 1682 a prisoner burnt the tolbooth door and escaped and a few weeks later another achieved freedom by breaking the lock on its replacement. In 1701 the jail was burned down by one of its inmates. The corner property behind the fountain was designed by A & W. Reid for the Royal Bank in 1856 and was extensively remodelled when acquired by its present owners Woolworth's in 1928.

Clarks
TO LET
OLIVERS
GRANADA

The Plainstones

The formation of an open-air exchange was first proposed by the Town Council in 1785 and the laying-out of the 'Plainstones' as it came to be known followed shortly thereafter. For many years the Plainstones was level with the roadway, until in 1953 it was raised to segregate it from the increasing traffic. The Plainstones was the venue for the Friday corn market and for the feeing markets.

The fountain, designed by Thomas McKenzie, was erected in 1846 to commemorate the introduction of piped water to the city, funds being raised through public subscription. Beneath it there was at one time, not inappropriately, a gents' urinal. By the 1880s this had come to be regarded as somewhat beneath the dignity of the city of Elgin. A petition for its removal described "its objectionable situation leading to disgusting exhibitions" used as it was "chiefly by street loungers and hangers-on". It was removed in 1886. A proposal in 1976 that, following the construction of the town's relief road, the centre might be made over to pedestrians only, finally bore fruit in 1995

GRANADA

Thunderton House

In medieval times this was the site of the Great Lodging, a royal residence with orchards and a bowling green. In 1707 it came into the possession of the Dunbars of Thunderton acquiring the name Thunderton House. In 1746 Bonnie Prince Charlie spent a few days here on his way to Culloden, taking ill, for which he was reportedly bled. His hostess on that occasion, Lady Arradoul, a devoted Jacobite is said to have been buried in the sheets her Prince had slept in. Following its sale to John Batchen in 1800 it was much reduced in size and in the years thereafter served a variety of functions, church, furniture warehouse, printing works, masonic lodge, aerated water factory and hotel. It is currently being used as a public house.

THUNDERTON
HOUSE

St. Giles from the west

The old church of St. Giles was surrounded by the parish burial ground. It was discontinued about the middle of the 16th century. When the foundations of the present church were being dug no fewer than 19 cartloads of human bones were driven off to the Cathedral burial ground and interred there. Some of the coffins turned up were said to have been "quite fresh and the bodies hardly decomposed." Some of the old stones covering the graves were used to make side pavements on the High Street. The burial ground was enclosed by a wall, stones from which were employed in the building of the Tollbooth in 1605.

2 hour
cleaning
TAXI
F38 DNS
Let
Pizza
RESTAURANT
MILLSHOP

High Street - west end

The building on the left with the curvilinear gable is the White Horse Inn, which dates from the 17th century, although the frontage is a reconstruction. In the early part of last century this was a much-frequented house presided over by the famous Elizabeth 'Lucky' Innes, celebrated by the local poet, William Hay, in the lines "*Her name is Mrs Innes and the White Horse is her sign, And happy is the man or beast that chances there to dine, For all her provender is good, her whisky, ale and wine.*" Adjoining the White Horse are the premises built for the Caledonian Bank about 1845 on the site of the 17th century Elchies House, at one time used as a boarding school for young ladies.

HIGHLAND HOME INDUSTRIES
MILLSHOP
SALE SALE SALE SALE
HALIFAX
Littlejohn's
F38 DNS

Royal Bank

This building was at one time the home of General Anderson, the founder of Anderson's Institution. After his death it was bought by the Commercial Bank who in 1852 took down the front of the house and rebuilt it in the Italianate style seen here. The sculptured female heads with floral wreaths between the first and second storey windows represent the four seasons. Only in the last two hundred years has the town's waste been carried away in underground sewers. Before then the 'common gutter' was an open sewer which ran between the Bank and the adjoining property carrying all the waste from the western part of the town down to the Lossie at Borough Briggs. In 1969 the Commercial Bank merged with Royal Bank who replaced this building with the present one in 1971.

radio
ENTALS.
TO LET
Enquiries to
CIRCUS
CIRCUS
ELGIN
ELGIN

Murdoch's Wynd

Blackfriars Wynd was one of the streets of medieval Elgin, leading to the monastery of the Black Friars. Later named Ragg's Wynd, it has been known as Murdoch's Wynd since the middle of last century. The building of the town's relief road from 1979-81 led to the almost complete obliteration of the street and its buildings. The Mission Hall, on the extreme left on the old photograph, was demolished in 1979 just a few weeks before its centenary.

40

Ladyhill Close / Ladyhill House

This picture shows the buildings of Ladyhill Close, demolished in 1974. In the background is Ladyhill House built by Robert Young in 1811 and much altered by the noted Elgin architect, Thomas Mackenzie, in 1853 with further additions by A Marshall Mackenzie in 1908. The elder Mackenzie collected many heraldic and sculptured stones from demolished buildings which he transferred to Ladyhill. In the present century it was the home of John Foster, author of 'The Bright Eyes of Danger', until his death in 1946 after which it had a succession of occupants before becoming an hotel in 1963.

Ladyhill

The 80 foot high column on the Ladyhill was erected in 1839 to the memory of George, 5th Duke of Gordon and has a wheel stair to the top. The statue of the Duke by the Elgin sculptor Thomas Goodwillie was not added until 1855. Ladyhill was the site of Elgin Castle, a Royal residence until 1297 and a fortress for at least 150 years after that. The Castle chapel was dedicated to St. Mary the Virgin hence the name Ladyhill. In 1784 a local inventor let off an air balloon from Ladyhill which, borne by a strong wind, vanished from sight over the hill of Pluscarden. It was said to have come down a large chimney in a neighbouring parish where the landlord was brewing whisky and, burning in the fire, destroyed the brew and scorched the legs of a girl warming herself by the hearth.

In 1870 a series of open air evangelistic services, drawing crowds of up to 2,000, were held here.

Dr Grays Hospital

In the foreground is the West End Fountain erected in 1892 by the Elgin Amenities Association for the benefit of cattle passing to market in Elgin from Alves, Pluscarden and Duffus. It was removed and replaced by a roundabout in 1949. The foundation stone of Dr Gray's Hospital was laid on the same day in 1815 that news of the Battle of Waterloo reached Elgin. Dr Alexander Gray was a native of Elgin, who did not get along with his wife. In his will he referred to her as "the most abandoned and deliberately infamous wife that ever distinguished the annals of turpitude." Not surprisingly then he left the bulk of his fortune, £20,000 for a hospital "for the sick of the poor in the town and county of Elgin". The building, designed by James Gillespie Graham of Edinburgh, occupies a commanding site at the west end of the town and was opened to patients in 1819. Part of Gray's bequest also included £2,000 for "the comfort of virgins whose hope had decayed" After a number of reworkings over the years, a brand new hospital was constructed behind the original building and opened in 1995.

Oakwood Motel

Opened in 1932 and believed to be the first motel in Scotland, the Oakwood's design was Canadian influenced. Originally a little rustic tea-room, the Oakwood became a favourite venue for Elginites on a summer afternoon and evening. The tea-room was extended to include a dance hall and lounge. There were also a caravan site, petrol pumps and a well with goldfish. The petrol pumps were "painted to represent trees and the supervening lights camouflaged as burning bushes", music poured "forth from the hillside from a hidden loudspeaker connected to a radio gramophone."

In 1935 the first of the wooden chalets was erected to be let for the sum of 6s 6d per night under the title Honeymoon Hotel. They were demolished just a few years before the Oakwood itself ceased trading at the end of 1994.

Sheriffmill

There has been a mill on this part of the River Lossie since 1237 when the Mill of Uchterspynie was erected on land granted by Bishop Andrew Moray to Walter de Moravia. It probably became known as the Sheriff's mill about the year 1300. The present building, now converted into a dwelling house, dates from the nineteenth century. For many years it was worked as a flour mill and then as a weaving mill under the ownership of one John Munro, tweed merchant and amateur magician, known as the 'Wizard of Moray'. Later still it was converted into an aerated water factory. The bridge was built in 1803 as part of the Aberdeen-Inverness turnpike and, unlike some others, survived the Great Flood of 1829. In 1959 the main trunk road was re-routed over a new bridge a little further upstream.

Oldmills

Oldmills is the oldest mill on the Lossie, so old that its origins cannot be determined. It was in Royal hands until 1230 and was granted to the monks of Pluscarden by Alexander II. Although originally a meal mill, it also served as a brewery in the 17th century, when there are references to brewers at Oldmills being censured by the Church for selling "aill in tyme of divine service". From at least the middle of the 13th century until 1821 those occupying the burgh lands were under obligation to have their grain ground at this mill on payment of the customary toll. In recent years the buildings and machinery have been restored to make a very attractive addition to Elgin's tourist attractions.

Blackfriars Haugh

In the 17th century the lands of Blackfriars Haugh were in the hands of a Sutherland family who dug up the foundations of the old monastery and removed gravestones for hearths in some houses they owned in Bishopmill. In 1851 "a commodious, substantial and elegantly finished mansion" was built for local lawyer William Grigor "near the old residence". In 1883 this house was replaced by the present one, built of Newton stone in the style of "an old baronial castle." It stands to the west of the site of the original monastery of Blackfriars erected in the 13th century. In 1946 the house was gifted to the town of Elgin by Mrs H C Bibby. In the years following it was used as a pre-nursing training centre and as accommodation for Elgin Academy. It is now one of the town's premier hotels.

Holy Trinity Church

Prior to the opening of North Street about 1821 the Episcopalians in Elgin worshipped in a chapel at 74 High Street. After this they resolved to build the present church, probably designed by William Robertson, and completed in 1826. Amongst the many alterations made since then have been the addition of a west wing in 1875 and of a commemorative porch to Colonel Forteath of Newton.

The church was built to close the view from High Street down North Street, a view since dislocated by the building of Alexandra Road and the insensitive sighting of street lighting.

BLACKFRIARS
Guest House
Bed & Breakfast
Evening Meal

Lossie Green

Lossie Green was Elgin's playground for many years until the opening of the Cooper Park in 1903 and although now largely given over to car parking is still the site for travelling amusements. In the background can be seen the old gasworks which were demolished in 1933 following the construction of new works in 1931. During the Second World War units of the Polish Army were encamped here. Drying clothes was a problem for those large numbers of Elgin folk who lived in the closes. The Town Council were at one time much concerned about the number who draped clothes and blankets over the fencing around the public park and clothes poles were erected on Lossie Green for public use. The ground here was levelled by the dumping of rubbish, a practice which was finally stopped in 1888.

Bishopmill Bridge

A two-arched bridge was constructed over the Lossie at Bishopmill in 1814, but being built on a gravelly foundation it did not survive the Great Floods of 1829. In 1831 it was replaced by this cast-metal bridge the iron-work for which was brought by sea from Aberdeen to Burghead. By 1871, this bridge had become too narrow for the increased traffic it was asked to carry. In that year a third and still surving bridge was built proving "a great comfort and convenience to the community, there being no bridge in the county which has so much traffic upon it." On its opening day it was tested by having a traction engine, ten loaded wagons and some two hundred people on it at one time. The movement of the bridge was said to be scarcely perceptible. This was a great improvement on the previous bridge which "trembles and shakes like an aspen leaf when a lorry or cart is on it".

In 1947 it was announced that the replacement of this bridge would be "delayed" and so it was until 1988 when the fourth Bishopmill bridge was opened. These photographs show the second and third bridges.

The Dry Bridge

About 1820 a new road was made from Elgin to Lossiemouth. Where it passed through the village of Bishopmill it was necessary to dig a deep cutting thus dividing Bishopmill High Street in half. The re-connection was made by means of this bridge, which since it had no water beneath it was known as the 'Dry Brig". It quickly became a nuisance, horses took fright at the overhanging bridge, cartloads of hay stuck in it and no traction engines could pass through it. By 1898 it' had become such an inconvenience to traffic that it was removed thus dividing the High Street of Bishopmill once more.

J.K. HENDERSO
RISING SUN
BAR

Elgin Tanworks

At the time it was destroyed by fire in February 1961 the Elgin Tanworks, though then in use as a wool store, was the oldest industrial building in use as such in the town, dating from the 17th century. The blaze, with flames shooting 70 to 80 feet in the air, reduced the building to rubble in the space of two hours despite the attentions of six fire brigades. In the 19th century the business was in the hands of the Culbard family who expanded their operations, both at home and abroad, until by the 1870s it was the largest north of Dundee. In 1966 a block of shops was opened on the Tannery site. These were later occupied by the furnishing retailers opposite after their premises burned down in 1984.

Deanshaugh Mill

In days gone by the waters of the River Lossie provided the power for such industry as there was in Elgin and a string of mills from Scroggiemill east to Sheriffmill, Oldmills, Bishopmill, Kingsmills and Newmill were located on its banks. At Deanshaugh John Ritchie, a local merchant, set up a mill for the processing of tobacco and linen and with machinery for bleaching, the field between the mill and Deanshaugh Bridge being used as the bleachfield. In the course of time this was superseded by a sawmill and a threshing mill which by the beginning of this century had also fallen into disuse. Now only vestiges of the workings remain to be seen.

Cooper Park

Grant Lodge and its grounds were given to the town of Elgin in 1902 by Colonel G A Cooper and opened as a public park in August 1903. The grounds were laid out to a design of A Marshall Mackenzie, a noted local architect, to include bowling green, tennis and croquet courts. The boating pond was originally intended as a skating rink with boating not introduced until the summer of 1923. The wall surrounding the park was largely removed and replaced by a "single rod of iron on iron posts, so planned that cattle cannot get access." However, in the early days the Town Council gained an income from letting the Park as grazing for sheep. As can be imagined this created some nuisance to the human users of the Park especially in the bandstand and the entrance porch to Grant Lodge, where the sheep used to shelter in wet weather. Vandalism was a problem in those days too. The imposition of Regulations was deemed necessary especially after "eighty young trees were seriously damaged by young men who ought to have known better". There were at one time a number of fruit trees in the Park, apples and pears available to anyone, with youngsters almost always the first on the scene, "with dire results to their digestive organs".

Grant Lodge

Grant Lodge was built about 1750 as the Elgin residence of the Earls of Seafield, and was enlarged a century later by Francis William the 6th Earl. By the time they were gifted to the town in 1902, the house and its grounds covered some 45 acres and included the sites of the town houses of the Marquis of Huntly and the lairds of Pluscarden and Dunkinty as well as the so-called Bishop's Palace. Since 1903 Grant Lodge has housed Elgin's public library. An election row between the Duff and Grant interests in 1820 brought 700 Highlanders of the Clan Grant marching to Grant Lodge to protect Lady Ann Grant. With the townspeople of Elgin armed in self-defence a pitched battle was narrowly avoided. This incident has gone down, somewhat grandiosely, as the 'last clan uprising in Scotland.'

ELGIN
PUBLIC
LIBRARY

Greyfriars Church

The Franciscans or Grey Friars, came to Elgin about the middle of the 13th century and established themselves on the south side of the High Street opposite the Little Cross. In the 15th century they moved to the present site. At the Reformation the property came into secular hands where it remained for some three centuries until purchased in 1891 by the Sisters of Mercy. With the buildings becoming too costly to maintain, the then Marquis of Bute came to the rescue and in 1896 commissioned John Kinross to restore the church. In September 1898 mass was celebrated here for the first time since the Reformation. The Sisters of Mercy had come to Elgin in 1871. The first convent was a small cottage near St. Sylvester's Hall. Later a few small cottages on the opposite side of Abbey Street were acquired and converted into a Convent. In 1872 the Sisters took charge of the present St. Sylvester's School. Later a number of branch houses were opened, in Keith, Tomintoul and, as late as 1968, in Buckie.

Greyfriars Street

Greyfriars Street was the site of the police office and prison from the middle of the 19th century until 1963 when the present police headquarters opened in Moray Street. The Greyfriars Street building was demolished in 1965. In the distance in the old photograph can be seen the last of Elgin's many malt kilns, now the site of a superstore. In early times there was a very extensive brewing trade in Elgin for which a number of malt kilns, each a stone-built, slate-roofed building about one hundred feet long were constructed. After the Union of 1707 brewing declined and the malt kilns found a new use as weaving sheds until that industry too declined in the early nineteenth century. Dominating the foreground of the contemporary photograph is the 1992 extension to the local authority's administrative headquarters.

Commerce Street

The crossroads at the top of Commerce Street was the site of the South or Smithy Port until it was removed in 1792. Hereabouts too were the Grammar and Sang Schools which gave Commerce Street its earlier name of School Wynd. The coming of the railway gave an enhanced status to this street as the principal entrance to the town from the railway stations. About 1857 a body composed of private individuals and local organisations bought up several properties and remodelled and widened the street. It was at this time that it was given the more dynamic name of Commerce Street to replace the old School Wynd.

ELGIN
NEXT

South Street

The section of South Street from Commerce Street to Batchen Street was the subject of a self-help regeneration scheme promoted by the Town Council in 1963. The Eagle Hotel was demolished in 1936 and superseded by the Argyle Buildings. The Grand Hotel next door was built on the site of the old Royal Oak Inn in 1898. Designed by Reid & Wittet it was the first public building in Elgin with neon lights. It functioned as an hotel until the 1950s when part of it was sold to form a new club-room for the Seaforth Club. In 1962 the remainder of the building was converted into flats with a bookshop and youth centre and renamed Emmaus House.

COMMERCE STREET
ANDREW BEGG
sale
sale
25

Fife Arms Close

Seen here is the Fife Arms Close at the top of which The Picture House built in the latter half of 1926. It had seating for over 700 and included in its original equipment a Mustel Celesta orchestral organ. The first film shown was 'Kiki' starring Norma Talmadge. It was here that the first talking picture in the north was screened, in 1930. That picture was 'Gold Diggers of Broadway' described as "one of the most amazing and gorgeous of all natural colour films'. The Fife Arms Inn had its origins in St. Duthac's manse, a resting place for pilgrims on their way to worship at the shrine of St. Duthac in Tain. In the early part of the last century it became the Fife Arms Inn with its stable buildings stretching back up the close to South Street. The stable buildings were replaced by the Lido Buildings, home of the Lido Cafe and palais de danse, about 1928.

P.L. Civiera
CALEY BINGO
One way
PICTURE HOUSE ELGIN
CHRISTIES
INTERFLORA

Town Hall

The Town Hall was opened by the Earl of Fife in 1885 when, in commemoration of the event, a medal was presented to each school pupil in the burgh, some 1300 in all. Designed by A. Marshall Mackenzie, the tower was 125ft high and the projecting keystones over the windows bore the sculptured heads of Apollo, Vulcan and Ceres. It was topped by the weathercock first erected in 1784 on the tower of the old Tolbooth, being removed when that building was demolished in 1843. At the time of its construction it was regarded as being "somewhat out of the way". Indeed there was a good deal of argument over whether the hall should be sited in Moray Street or closer to the town centre in Commerce Street. A fire in the afternoon of December 11th 1939 reduced the building to rubble in the space of a few hours, with a strong breeze, lack of water pressure and the varnished pitch pine interior proving too much for the fire-fighters. The roof of the main hall fell in within an hour with the massive tower following soon after. Since 1963 the site has been occupied by the local police headquarters.

Police
G463 MYS

Highland Railway Station

The Inverness & Aberdeen Junction Railway opened from the Highland capital to Elgin in March 1858. The first excursion trains made the trip in a little under two hours. In addition to the main station buildings on the north side, a wooden shed was erected on the south side as winter shelter for passengers going north. Elgin's station facilities were the subject of many complaints over the years, the most recent campaign resulting in a new station opening in 1990. The old photograph shows the station specially decorated for the visit, (her one and only) of Queen Victoria in September 1872. She stayed for about seven or eight minutes and never left the train.

Elgin

Laichmoray

The Railway, later Station Hotel, was built in 1853 for the Morayshire Railway Company. It was described at the time as "commodious and splendid", "elegantly finished ...with plate glass" with stabling for 16 horses and a half covered veranda fronting the two main public rooms. The closure in 1874 of Weston House School left a gap in Elgin's educational facilities. As a result the Elgin Educational Institute Ltd was formed to provide education "for the sons of the better classes." The Station Hotel was acquired and a series of large school rooms added to its east side, but by 1879 the Institute was forced into liquidation and the buildings sold to Robert Hay, cabinetmaker. It became the Station Hotel once more until the late 1950s when it was renamed the Laichmoray Hotel.

GNSR Station

The Morayshire Railway, opened from Elgin to Lossiemouth in 1852 was, despite being several years in the completion, still the earliest north of Aberdeen. It was not without its teething troubles: on the opening run the train was over 15 minutes late on a 15 minute trip due to the "newness and stiffness of the locomotive." Its station at Elgin was "completely metamorphosed" in 1863 when links were established with the Great North of Scotland Railway's line from Aberdeen. In 1881 the Morayshire and the Great North were formally amalgamated, an event soon followed by the opening of another line into Elgin, that along the coast from Portsoy. After many delays this station was replaced by a new one. Completed in 1902 it is now a business centre housing the offices, amongst others, of the local Enterprise Company.

Duff Avenue

Duff Avenue was formed in 1895 on land belonging to the Elgin Guildry Fund Society and was named after their President, Dr George Duff. For many years after the Reformation the Catholics in Elgin had no proper place of worship. In 1827 John Forbes was appointed priest. He travelled extensively in Britain and abroad raising funds for the erection of a church. So successful was he that work began in 1843 on a design by local architect, Thomas Mackenzie, which was opened for worship as St. Sylvester's Church in the following year.

C963 TRS

New Elgin

New Elgin was founded in 1830 as "a working men's suburb". Following the opening of the Morayshire Railway in 1852, the village began to grow and in 1853 a group of villagers came together to form an unofficial town council. One of their first acts was to raise the money, 8s 9d, to buy a drum and appoint a town drummer to beat the drum every weekday morning at 5 a.m. to awaken the inhabitants. The first drummer was a veteran of the Battle of Waterloo.

By 1879 it was said that "the houses are in general tolerably good, but occupied, with few exceptions, by the humbler classes." In 1888 a water supply for the village was opened although it was reported that very little water was drunk at the opening ceremony. Improvements to the pavements in 1934 meant that motorists no longer had to contend with pedestrians walking along the crown of the main street. The village has expanded greatly in recent years as a suburb of Elgin.

Select Bibliography

Cramond, W. ....The Records of Elgin. 2v. 1903-07

Elgin Society ....Historic Elgin and its Cathedral. 1974

Elgin Society ....Old Elgin. 1946 + 1954

Mackintosh, H.B. ....Elgin Past and Present. 1914

Mackean, C. ....The District of Moray. 1987

Seton, M. ....Elgin Past and Present. 1980

Seton, M. ....Elgin In Old picture Postcards. 1983

Watson, J.&W. ....Morayshire Described. 1868

Wyness, F. ....Mediaeval Elgin. 1944

Young, R. ....Annals of the Parish and Burgh of Elgin. 1879

Elgin Courant 1836-1967

Elgin Courier 1827-34, 1845-74

Northern Scot ....1880 to date